CARBON ATOM

". . If tributes cannot

be implicit,

give me diatribes and the fragrance of iodine . ."

(Marianne Moore)

CARBON ATOM

Alexander
Hutchison

LINK-LIGHT
Glasgow
2006

First published 2006

LINK-LIGHT

47 Camphill Avenue
Langside
Glasgow G41 3AX

ISBN 0-9554434-0–7
978-0-9554434-0-4

Printed and bound in Scotland
by Pace Print Ltd, Edinburgh

Contents

1

2

3

Acknowledgements

CARBON ATOM

1

AN OUNCE OF WIT
TO A POUND OF CLERGY

Let's begin our panegyric: weft of wool
and warp of cotton. Tow a drogue at your stern
so you won't broach to. Abandon your tails
and cheek pouches. For loft, for distance
put the baffy back in your bag.

.

Who wants this mush of meat and fat: poets
of the pemmican (dried and pounded) school –
with bugger the berry to give it some taste?

Where it's grind me to powders, and cankering
creeds – with never a blink of primrose banks
never a hint of beech woods building.

.

Strip off your rags and bend the bow.
Get your ordinance full and flowing.

.

And scrape me rather some pepperpots of potency:
the grains of Paradise, the cubeb, the chili
the cayenne of Guinea, the pods of Sichuan.

.

Put worms to work, and moles to mark them.

.

I'd have us smile like a parcel of seraphs.
Not lolloping loose; not dying duckies.

Ladies in sable, come up, come in –
take the weight off your feet, take ease
of all your rasping parts.

.

Warty newts and fire-bellied toads
continue your aquatic and sociable ways.
Natterjacks of heathland and dunes (your loud
rolling call like a ratchet). Corncrake
of bogland and grasses; fugitive, invisible.

.

Aspect of all aslip and aslither: things
that tremble, things athwart. Come gastropods
come snails and limpets – sallow, blanch
and black-avisèd.

.

Things that scuttle, that squeal, or puff
themselves up, or launch themselves through
the air at intruders.

.

Take root all sprouts of *pseudoplatanus*.
Protophytes and protomorphs, let's get a move on.
With hooks and burrs and green helicopters.

.

Set with ardour bright and clear
beams, jambs, lintel and moulding:
an architrave of red-hot promise.

.

Eager and apt we bristle, we burgeon.

The hand of the glazier puts putty to the frame.
The pastry-cook pounds out his faintest concoction.

.

Knit up the bones of computation.

Let like kiss like.
Let bright affinity walk
in anklets of amber, in fillets
of silver.

.

Not ten go, but twenty posts out of your way.

.

Cool and open and tempting the vista.
The spiral of the condor vast and leisurely.
The bat at noon (anomalous) in twittering loops.

.

Let all things fused
transparent, opaque
enjoy diversity.

Snaps and scraps of quick allurement.

.

Stone-crop in succulent rosettes
of yellow-pink and crimson-green.

.

Penetration of the optic:
when all the down-draft of wintry webs
is wafted away.

.

O, the women in dove-grey
swimming suits!

the roundel windows
admitting the light of day.

WEST COAST TALLY

"Cha'n uaisle duine na cheird"

Torridon: start with
rock split and the rowan
growing out of it – after all
that's right in front of my nose.

Lochinver: I thought he
was the Devil himself – clever
wicked, affectionate, haughty.

Bernera: not quizzical
insistent – with courage
and *largesse.*

Braes: words and wood.
No man above his trade – but
this one lofty, familiar: beyond
Cuillin ridge his line across the sky.

ALBA

'Foedum' Tacitus said
the weather was. Well
better the weather foul
than the will
of the people.

LADY SCOTTER

Lady Scotter
had a daughter

used to swim
just like an otter

sleek and quick
along the river

so it made the
young men quiver.

Not the sort of
thing that Scotter

quite approved
of in a daughter.

SPARKS IN THE DARK

Alice Pleasance Liddell
Interrupted some boys in mid-piddle.
"Desist, louts," said Alice,
"Or each tiny phallus
Will spark in the dark on my griddle."

EPITAPH FOR A BUTCHER

Noo he's safely doon below,
They'll no mak puddens o Mr. Snow.
For loin o pork and gigot chop
The wifies cam in croods tae shop.
A always fancied (some fowk didnae)
Sweetbreads, ox-tongue, tripe and kidney.
Nane criticized his potted heid;
But *contra mortem* nae remeid.

JIMP

Jimp she was:
neat as a needle;
sprightly, lively
slender as grass

EXCUSE ME FOR SAYING SO

But you look like Tuesday
was payday, and Monday had never
come. Like your backside has been slung
out the window for the last half hour.
Like you just met your wife and overtime
arm in arm. Like the car keys are in your golf
bag and the golf bag's in the river. Like your
plumber's helper just got pulled in by the police.

Aye, and you look like your nose was stripped
and varnished by mistake. Like crowdie was called
for, and mousetrap is all there is. Like someone
put the polish to your socks and not your shoes.
Like the cat crept under your duvet and farted.
Like somebody coughed in your soup.

ANNOUNCEMENT

Ladies and gentlemen,
may I have your attention please?
This train is approaching Silence station.

Passengers may alight here for connections to Gasp,
Dither, Lilac, Bobbinquaw, Jawbone, Sundry, Zipper.
Passengers may also connect to Freshet, Raddle,
Bolus, Reptile, Grout.

Passengers may change for Lucrece, Posy, Quillet,
Yammer, Darkness, Greater Dark.
Also for Soth, Sarlic, Hope, Love, Treacle.
Also for Radisson, Palgrave, Salient, Fly-boy.

They may also change for Christabel and Falssemblant,
with a further connection to Daphnis and Chloe.

Passengers are requested to check items of luggage
and all personal belongings before leaving the train.
Passengers with guide dogs should note that the platform
will be available on the left-hand side.

This train will be arriving at Silence in a few
minutes' time.

Thank you.

BY THE BEEF
AND NOT TOUCHING IT

1

Crows on the roof

some starlings nesting
under the eaves –

gangway for racketeers
black and green and
glossy.

All of a dither
epiplectic as usual

not much to the ditty
whaup whaup.

.

Raucous and ready
with the slant remark

wide open by nature
to the cutting return.

2

Gauche, giddy, gruff
in a byway below

the confluence of folk –

like a basket of cats
at a festival bonfire

glowering and glozing.

.

From jangle and spit
to pork chops and
synagogues.
.

Cannonades
of amorous glances.

3

Old agony bags
the butcher's dog

is out for a stroll.

His eye would blench
the regard of eagles

his insides chirming
like finches in a pot.

4

Bring your backsides
to an anchor! – loud hail
from a foul corner –

sit down and give
us some news.
.

From croodling
and crinkling

slap-bang
into bafflement.
.

(A lovely fellow
really –

took his black drop
like a gentleman

half way between
the transit of Venus
and Mercury.)

5

I'm a pantologist
Lancelot says

I know everything.

My brother
was a pantomancer

she comes back:

couldn't for the life
worm his way into
socks.

.

*Whaup whaup
wheedle deedle.*

6

A pretty
cynomorphic

observation

on her part though
if you ask me.

Striking it off
like a damp match
on sandpaper.

Everybody gawping.

7

Took his black
drop (as mentioned)

just like a gentleman

hardly knew
what hit him

or how high up.
.

Some kind
of imaginary

disgruntlement
most likely.
.

The last thing
she growled:

*Put that
serpent away.*

MIND THE GAP

Of course there is an error
in the cleanness of the sea, and
for the landing of eggs outside the
compound something must be done.
Whereas tea and honey are merely
in decline, the lemon slice has
taken a holiday and may not return.

The wind in the chestnut trees
I assume has been taken for granted.
Conversely, firing of the jackhammer
at 7.15 occupied my full attention.

It is not that the women are not
wonderful – they are – but that
they are out of the question.
Elżbieta in particular has
legs that go nowhere.

What is the matter with the
butter on that dish? Is it possible
I will forget the mixing of cement
that followed my early re-awakening?

Agnieszka could have been more
pleasant in a number of respects –
nevertheless, her lower lip has a
quality I do not discount: that is
as far as pinkness and durability
are concerned.

Can no one here fix a proper
time for appointments? The canal
is empty; the remaining ducks
are in a state of confusion.

As for myself, I would
take a tram. But number 6
runs away; whereas 13 and 12
come together, overcrowded with
unpleasant people.   It is risible
what the taxi driver has suggested.

Well, nothing could be
further from the truth. I did try
the scrambling of egg; still the
marmalade was beyond my grasp.

What does Bożena think
she is up to? When she dances
it is plainly disconcerting.
Perhaps we should all sit down.

No it is not my turn.
I think after all there was
something funny about that slice
of sausage. Whatever unravelling
you had in mind will probably
now have to be postponed.

Disappointment is everywhere;
but when notice is short, displays
of pique are not unforeseen. Adjik
has gone off at a tangent once more.
What happened to his finger is no
longer our concern. I suspect the
biscuits have gone off with him too.

Unfold the map, and re-affix
the dog. Perhaps the jam will work.
I did spot some pickles and preserves
in the cupboard in the bathroom.

Port side is always best.
On the green part there is nothing
that will serve. If it comes to that,
take care to salute the quarterdeck
when piped on board. All hands take
great offence if this be neglected.

LAST TIME

The last time I saw him
he was loath to take
his eyes off two frigorific
local fillies, pacing along
the Coogait – half way
between Bannister's bar
and the mortuary gate.

COUNCIL DEBATE RESUMES

Like some beetle stranded
on its back, which with a
sudden twist, a jerk, flips
front and forwards on its
face again – elated, frisky
the provost picked up his
fankled thread once more

THE HAT

I thought I saw you.
I thought I could see you
come in and wander round –
I thought I recognized the hat.

Wherever it is you've clambered
off to, is there anyone there
to twist a story, lift a dram?

I could have sworn it was you –
my hand is out – even now I'm
smiling, waiting to say hullo.

CITRONELLA

Lemon
sponge she
used to make

with lemon
butter icing.

I could think
of worse things

than sinking
in again to that
light sponge
astringent icing

the length
of those cool
dark citrus
afternoons.

SIBILANCE: SWIFTS

Erratic, headlong
sibilant: swifts are hinges
creaking in the air.

BRIEF PRAISE POEM
for *EM*

Who dives deeper
into the darting
shoal of words,

and who draws
a sweeter draught
from Mungo's well?

DIDN'T DO
(for Norman)

Well, I'll tell you
what he didn't do:

he didn't have a neat
wee cunt and push it around;

he didn't lean on – or into –
not for a sense of *obligation*;

he didn't smear all over
like old tar on foreshore rocks;

he measured by what he admired
not by what he might get;

he thought there was more
to life than passable dentition;

he sometimes snarled and sometimes sneered
– but never at next door neighbours;

If he cosied up anywhere
he did it because he liked it;

he didn't say "ah hah hah" out
loud in buses just to draw attention;

he opted for chins and buttercups
rather than 'a forest of symbols';

his bucket always reached down
to the water in the well;

what it took he knew –
what it took to know he loved.

AINCE WUID, AN AYE WAUR

The dreary boys, the weary boys
the boys that canna go –
Scrunty hens roon but-an-bens,
the quines that winna show.

Nae lowpin jauds, bit driddlan
slaw – wi skeel an skilp agley.
Mochie, moosy, mizzelt for nowt
fan aa the jaa gings by.

It's hit the bar or hit the fleer –
("By Christ, this sawdust's nice, eh?)
It's stirks an stovies: "Stookie, yer oot.
Nae need t' speir ye twice, eh?"

Aa yon thirled, bunsucken crew
that quidna cock an crank it:
wid raither jook, or mooch a fry
or draw yer bleed an bank it.

For dreary boys an weary boys
nae wappens in the schaw –
An aul wanthriven carlin, chiels,
is aa ye'll clip an claw.

THE POET'S ADVICE TO HIMSELF

Hink, swink, swipe and swish:
Swizzeld, swyvit, swanny;
When the great aul Wife steps
Doon tae pish – ye'd better
Shift it Sauney!

ANNALS OF ENLIGHTENMENT

Hume passes
into the absolute,
brace-girdled, without
concern.

    James,
laird of Auchinleck,
as this transpires, lays
boisterous breath along
his doxy's shoulder,

elevates the skirt,
and takes her on the dust
of a stonemason's table,
some way below
the Castle hill.

.

In or out
of armour, which
would you rather –

cool release
of the *bon philosophe*
or Boswell's perturbation?

Much to be endured,
and little to be enjoyed?

or what mix in between?

.

At ten, a drum
for clart and creesh
on close and vennel.

The wind
in a shift lifts
leaves along old
Calton wall.

PEA AND HAM

Like they were baith hunkert
in Hungrie Mary's kitchy,
someplace in Dundee –
suppin deid man's face soup
wi lang drappin jaas.

UNFINISHED BUSINESS
for *C.M.G.*

The first door cracked back, and there they lay:
scummers of pots and flayers of horses; jaws that clamp,
words that stink; flowery potatoes boiled in their jackets;
dabblers in cytoplasm, dacoits and daddy-long-legs;
virtual realtors gazumping like crazy; rooks crok-crocking
from the tippy-tops of trees:

> Idle or daedal –
> which is it to be?

iron pumpers, counter jumpers, carpet fitters bristling
with a mouthful of tacks; tomcats, corncrakes, cute
bicuspids; all the little shining ones; all those that
would grudge you one jowl of the bell.

The second door swung, so more became clear:
tethered tups; tattered drapes; the slalom boys of Dandruff
Canyon; phagocytes, phylacteries, *polski ogorki*; the exhalation
of piled-up corpses; beaters of candy floss, fairground artists;
earnest persuaders with the integrity of tissue paper;
all those women who run as though their feet were on
strings instead of on legs; all those shrubs pruned
too soon and suffering die-back.

Shoulder to the third door, and as you would expect:
sweet saurian smilers; choppers and changers;
men in blue corduroy, ladies in jumpers; brandy bumpkins
buttered and bandy; r.p. flannel dunkers; polymathic magpies;
pertinacious prognosticators holding their noses; shit that sells,
bugs that burn; bellhops, cowflops, moderate restrainers;
tourists in chaps and spurs lining the fire break;
piners, whiners, dainty dinahs:

> (as gentle a set of worms
> as you are like to see)

here-I-come, hempseed, listless rival:
death's on the whistle like the wind through trees.

Round the corner and down the stairs:
polyglot cocksuckers; chirpy charmers; porkers and moochers:
bracken for breakfast, neighbours for lunch. Last but not
least: flies in putty; wise guys and warblers; sad wicks
in seas of wax.

Coda: Scrape it if you like into one big bag-pudding (plums,
suet, orange peel); simmer it slowly, and serve it in slices:
who's to say it won't last for years?

THE HOLT
(for Ian)

Sinuous
from shadow

unsheathed
and silver

no pounce-work
no grudge music

words are in
the breathing ground

this uncircum-
scribable air

INCANTATION

– beginning with a couplet from *Carmina Gadelica*
   and with grace notes from the same source.

I have a charm for the bruising
a charm for the blackening
a charm for cheats and impostors.

I summon from the cold clear air
from the bare branches of the trees
from worms coiling under the ground –

charm against cruel intent
charm for neglect
charm against wicked indifference:

may it lie on the white backs of the breakers of the sea
may it lie on the furthest reaches of the wind.

A salve for those who would grudge against the poor
a salve for those who would harry the innocent
a salve for those who would murder children:

may it lie in the stoniest stretches of the hills
may it lie in the darkest shelving along the shore.

A salve for those that would cram
whatever life they have with possession –
for the rage of owning without entitlement
for the desperate murderous possession of things:

may it lie on the cloud-banks that range across the sky
may it lie on the face of Rannoch Moor in its remoteness.

A charm against mystification by doctors
a charm against deception by the self-appointed
a charm against horrific insistence:

from the breeze that stirs the last of the yellowing leaves
from the slanting of the sun as it falls through the window.

a salve against grasping
a salve against preaching
a salve against promises exacted by threat.

> Grace of form
> grace of voice
> grace of virtue
> grace of sea
> grace of land and air
> grace of music
> grace of dancing.

A salve against the uselessness of envy
a salve against denial of our own best nature
a salve against bitter enmity and silence.

> Grace of beauty
> grace of spirit
> grace of laughter
> grace of the fullness of life itself.

A salve to bind us
a salve to strengthen heart and happiness:

may it lie in the star-blanket there to spread over us
may it lie in the first light at the waking of day.

CARBON ATOM

2

SCOTA AND GAETHELOS

Scota:

I'll start on the day when
we sailed away from the court
of my father. My husband the one
whose tongue unlocked the sense
of other voices. I must say he was
as much a wonder to me as I was
apparently to him. What he saw
then I don't recall; I just know
I wanted the same.

The sea is like mother-of-pearl.
The sky is pearl and blue and
silver. My face is turned to you
as the light wind shifts and lifts
the sail. We have all our best
people with us. Gaethelos, tell
me, what name shall we give
to this broad sea?

Send out your best constructed
thought to the star that takes us
home. You seem to me like a
green straight stem spilling light
into the air around you. There's
the tide. Have we all the casks
and gear on board? You be
the sheet and I'll be the tack.
The wind will hardly know
what to make of us.

Gaethelos:

Let me speak, for pity's sake.
I have a great burst of words
inside me. Nimrod's tower was
never as bad as this. What's going
on? I don't want the past pursuing
me. Sometimes my blood boils up
like a campfire pot. It's never
going to stop; and the only
thing that holds it back
is Scota's voice.

Sometimes I think she sees
another person altogether; like
I think she sees another person
now. The ship will do. I know
the blood that waits ahead.
Whether the boys will do is
another question. They'll have
to. I'll just keep sending them
back in until they do.

I was never one to say: wait
three days, deliberate; when you
get a bone sniff it first. I had
a dream last night of a bird
that gleamed above a mountain
I never knew. The air was damp:
not dry, no dust, no sand at all.

I cannot understand: she sees
me pure – aye, no, not chaste –
she sees the thing that drives
me, and she knows that I would
put a flame to anything at all.
She knows that. Love, stay that
side. I'll take the windward rope.

Tongue, temper, ever reined
in, couldn't say. Whatever we
do it'll have her name. Whatever
that green place I'll maybe
soar and see it too.

COUP DE FOUDRE

There once were some people
who lived in a wood. And they
were shiny, shiny, shiny.
And the wood was special too.

Piece by piece they would
have the wood for themselves.
Only shiny ones could enter,
and shiny is for sure as shiny does.

One day each bole and crown
was ash – each branch and bud
(*tsk tsk*) – and all from a smidgen
of durable fire lobbed
in from the dusty beyond.

HEADING IN
TO THE BAR

Strike a lout
and you'd better
strike home.

> Keep the moon
> from the dogs;
> keep the bairns
> off the biscuit

What a terrible
face to wear
for a wedding!

> (Don't show that
> tooth if you don't
> mean to bite.)

A stone on your
cairn – sharp Murdo
might add –

> *Clach air*
> *do chàrn.*

Or – as
my New Jersey
companion was given
to venture:

> *No suckers?*
> *No nuts?*

SIMPLY PLATONIC

Because a harmony has no part in the inharmonical

     nor the swallow, nor yet the hoopoe

their several affections, active and passive, were all for the best

     whether essence of equality, beauty, or anything else

wrapped in a goatskin or some other disguise

     like the sound of the flute in the ears of the mystic

the terrible nature of her confinement

     although not the same as oddness

is not dissolved or decomposed at once.

(Selections from: *The Trial and Death of Socrates*)

KANTICLE

Since space is not a composite

    even poisons have their use

changing its meaning to suit our convenience

    resting reason on empty figments of the brain

the elimination of all personal freedom

    a world of the senses and a world of the understanding

would have to be an intuition

    sometimes covered with fruit sometimes with ice or snow

some transcendental ground of appearance

    the idea always true in itself.

(Selections from: *The Critique of Pure Reason*)

RHETORICAL DEVICES

Serious or trivial, just or unjust

      people must be kept on good terms

self-sufficiency is also a good –

      aptitude to learn, quick wits

the more so the more memorable

      games, relaxation and sleep.

Being able to be mocked, and mocking with grace

      they also nourish suspicions

if one thing is possible, then so is the other

      like dogs biting on stones

but not touching the one that throws them

      a kind of communal expediency

the same thing threatens them both.

(Selections from Aristotle: *The Art of Rhetoric*)

EPISTEMOLOGY

Kept on a short leash

      or smothered in many blankets

perception has this inexhaustible profundity

      a particular instance of rendering thanks

a pouring on of water.

How is it accomplished?

      assessment of plausibility

is as it is and not some other thing

      a stick to feel one's way in the dark

"one cannot speak of dogs without

      having a word for them" –

roots of this perversion go deep.

Yet all this is beside the point

      like brewing or pottery

stones fell because their end was downwards

      beyond expression of a sentimental attachment

a name, an image, a shadow

      the baby given to the breast

restlessness in sleep.

(Selections from *Meaning*: Polanyi and Prosch)

RECEIPT

It is an ideal occupation for children

       on a wet afternoon

put them head to tail in an oven proof dish

       and remove any pips

score as above or into little bars

       do not roll for this also toughens

cover with foil with a weight on top

       wrap the birds in the bacon rashers

melt the fat in a saucepan

       turn over when little bubbles appear

whip the egg whites very stiff

       then coat the other side

take out with a perforated spoon

       add watercress, fried oatmeal or skirlie

when cut it is a soft pink butter

       the gravy is served separately.

(Selections from *A Taste of Scotland*)

MAO AND THE DEATH OF BIRDS

Because they took, he thought,
more than their fair share of grain,
Mao decided the birds must die.

It could be this embraced concern
for the common weal, but economics
has its own imperative.

How did they do this?

Well, all one day, as long as it took,
the people banged on pots and pans
– whatever withering cacophony
they could raise – to keep the birds
aloft. Denied a roost, they flew until
their wings could not support them.
The people gathered every one
and put the pots to other use.

Was this not fine? The people, thus
instructed, dined on all that died.
Mao might have smiled; and no doubt
gathered in his own fair share.

Next year, without the birds,
the insects all enjoyed a carnival
in turn. The harvest failed –
and failed again – until in millions
people died. Was this not then
resoundingly complete?

What Mao had to say when
all transpired, again, I must regret,
I have no note; but do recall
another claim he brought – with pride –
of intellectual numbers down: 'more
than any Emperor that came before'.

How that was done was less
spectacular than what removed our
feathered friends – merely
another bland imperative.

At least they didn't cook
them where they fell – he probably
would draw the line at that.

When arbitrary despots rule, we
all are thralled to blind obedience.
Innocent and ignorant the Chinese people
died; and songs and words of those they
killed will come again – though in
what form is hard to say.

But may some demon boil the bones
of Mao in Yangtse's seething flood
for evermore – with everlasting
death to his vainglory.

CUNTY FINGERS

I didn't say it in
the first place, though
I knew what was up:
butter and toast – fingers
of toast – no, I hadn't seen
it before, but I wasn't
sure if I liked it.

I didn't say anything
to her when it surfaced
again – and I couldn't say
if she smiled or not. She
cleared the plate, not me.

HIPPERTIE-SKIPPERTIE

Hippertie-skippertie, heid lik a bee,
Bizzin roon fae flooer t' tree.
Kirr an kittle, come ower t' me,
Hippertie-skippertie, heid lik a bee.

ABOVE STROMNESS
for *GMB*

Mist at midnight,
night-scented stock;

happily betrayed
in what we choose
to name or work:

in this case gilly-
flower cruciferous
in clove-scented air.

YEEAIOW

The cat comes in
disappointed that she
can't come in next door.

She strokes around and
exits. She's right of
course: it's getting in
where you want that
urges the purr
properly on its way.

True desire or true
necessity goes unsounded
here – though what
she wants is what
she gives voice to.

It's only fat-tail
off in a huff
to sit down outside
in the hall attempting
to disguise a further
disappointment in the
last little while.

PHYTOGENY

If I were a tree I'd be ancient:
girth increases; growth rings get narrower.
Canopy reduced as new wood steadily declines.
Then fungi come to hollow heart-wood;
lichen splash gardens on broken stumps beyond.
Retrenchment may go on and on
before sparse living crown declares decay.

Like a tree too I am become in this state
more attractive to other forms of life.
The fungi of course;
but *saproxylic* insects fancy me as well: sipping
or scuttling wherever they may.
Rare and uncommon beetles line up to take their turn.
In and around the root *mychorrhizae* engage themselves in ways
I'm not exactly anxious to enquire.
Mosses, ferns and *bryophytes* compete to keep me green.

"People are naturally drawn" –
it says right here – "to big old trees."
"Tenacious, timeless .."
Phosphor at sunrise (Venus
the morning star)
silently combusts.

"Spirited though in decline" I'd say.
And best – as may hap – the whispering
below still clear
despite some flutterings above

CARBON ATOM

*"Now we are among the two innermost electrons of the carbon atom.
They mark out in their dance a neat sphere of electric charge. The four outer
electrons of carbon can come and go, whether in flame, in diamond,
or in DNA. But these inner electrons remain indifferent to ordinary experiences,
which cannot disturb their seclusion; they respond only to the nucleus within."*

A lightning strike can knock us off our stride,
Or radiation shifting in the sun's inside.

Make it ten to the power of three or four
and now you're talking: nerve enough to tap
"excuse me" on the perfect floor or plane
and swerve us into something special
not – *da capo* – same old stuff again.

We don't have much to do
with light that's visible: only
the rays that Roentgen
gazed straight through.

We never court seclusion.
What appears indifference may be misconstrued.
We do not sport the peacock flashiness of those lewd
variable neighbours in the outer port:
turning to fossil fuel or jewels or life.

Here in the inner ring just through the wall
our symmetry our charge our dance is all.
Nor strength nor love nor poison prove.
The core alone can stir us to remove.

NO, NO

Oh, no no no –
no – I wouldn't say
that – not hyenas.

No – no; well, not
exactly. I mean there
was the living body
they inherited –
there was that –
and what they later
got up to.

But – *no* – hyenas
is a bit strong –
wouldn't you say?
Just a touch.

GRASS OF LEVITY

Grass of levity
Span in brevity
Flower's felicity
Fire of misery
Wind's stability
Is mortality.

Simple utility
Fingered lubricity
Sprung from audacity
Known for rapacity
Any capacity
Is mortality.

Boundless servility
Neighbouring nillity
Primping polity
Bits of carnality
Vanity vanity
Is mortality.

What doesn't signify
Render or simplify
Impaled and crucified
Sat down or sanctified
Any identity
Is mortality.

Further and further space
Gruesome and human face
Graceless or born to grace
Here in this little space
Light in our little case
Is mortality.

[The first stanza is Anonymous and dates to 1609]

SHE SAID

Your man fed
the birds in Ire-
land – or so
the story goes.

Finches, robins:
taught them to
come to his hand.

For all I know
he could have
led them in
snatches of song.

When he left,
the cat made
short work of

all their whistly
perplexities.

A SATURNO CONDITUM

My friend, across the space
within this ancient hill-top town
everything gives breath to what
we wish or might aspire to.

Whatever the Volscians, whatever
those who built Cyclopic walls
before them felt, we feel.

Seeking beyond beauty or
ambition one at least to share
'an unguarded joke'
fireflies at night.

Hospes et humus – guests
a little while then gone.

.

Broom, elder, lemon-flower
the fragrance of valerian.

All this in a loom of light
is shuttled back and forth.
Swifts and martins carve the air.
Each olive tree on every
slope is shaped to give its
tiny blue-green song of praise.

LANDING

The trouble
with heaven
is no passion

.

the trouble
with hell
is no love

.

In that case pure Purgatory
would seem to be
the best place to alight

.

trimming
the birches

skimming
the reed-beds

to splash-down

and shaking
the water from
our wings

HOLE HOUSE FARM

The children
have got a bonfire going
in the back garden.

4 potatoes 3 eggs
and next to no idea
of how to go about it.

Three sheep
with long tails
in the middle distance
crunch their way
towards me.

Rain spots down;
the evening cools
to grey and green.

.

If I were to say
to you my heart is
like a log on fire

it wouldn't be true
not even close

but the nearest
thing I have to love is
this – is you – here
even when
the desperate animals

interrupt and some
dog makes the mistake
of barking all
strangers away.

CARBON ATOM

3

EPISTLE FROM PEVKOS

for Gael Turnbull

1

Gael, the bougainvillea here sends greetings in the deepest
cloudy pink. Hibiscus too at the kitchen window – blatant
scarlet. Along the lanes nearby: acacia, almond, oleander,
fig. A full-blown date palm occupies the yard next door.
All round the house low grapevines trail a welcome.
Anna our kindly Pevkian *ya-ya* calls to water them first thing.

Behind the town the mountain ridge is grey and arid,
Pecked and holed like tufa. At night in the starry dark
it looms at our back as banks of cloud.

2

Twice or thrice a day the steep down shelving
blue *thalassa* laps us round. Staying afloat's no
bother here: the briny deep can raise us up
in temperatures equivalent to bliss.

Anyone would want to swim in this,
whether they could swim or no.

3

A glass-bottomed boat took us round today to Lindos
over reefs that looked much closer than they were.
We knew when the sea was blue below it stretched
at least to fifteen fathoms. Iannis joked: "I lost my last
boat here. No problem. Only foreigners aboard".

The over-plump industrialist astraddle the prow
shows a good profile, and tries to look meagre
for his super-model squeeze or *lumber* (a Glasgow
term – like *pony* in West Clare). She is lissome
enough: complaisant, blonde and cocoa-tanned.
One-piece ebony swimsuit narrowly vee-ed.
Elegant pelvis; fine long femurs tapering down.

We squeaked a couple of times between
close pock-marked cliffs. I'm trying to think
of what might catch the texture of those rocks.
Exaggerated ash and pumice. Pinnacles and crevices.
Pachyderm sponge cake iced with $H_2 SO_4$.

The rest of the passengers undemonstrative.
Not many fish in evidence underneath: some
dots and splinters, intermittent shoals.

4

In my hand this postcard of four women gathering thin
corn or dried grass stalks for plaiting. They work a line
on a high headland with the sea behind them. One wears
a short straw bonnet against the sun. Others have white
headscarves wound round so little of their faces and none
of the neck or throat shows. It's not enough to say that
it must be hot work. They wear shirts, skirts, aprons
and dresses of blue, grey, pink and white, with further
binding to protect the skin at their forearms and wrists.

It could be Rhodes; it might be Orkney, or fields above
Cullen, after a dozen years of sudden climate change.

They must pause and stretch, bind with some wisps
and stoop again. Although they are posed and angled
here a little, you can imagine it anytime, almost anywhere.
It looks too hot for casual chat. A word or two perhaps
on a longer easing stretch – anything else held
back for whatever break they get and when.

5

Stepped out the kitchen door to re-arrange laundry
draped in the sun and found when I came back in a cicada
just inside on the terracotta coloured floor. The cicada is
light brownish-grey with tiger striping atop his back propelling
legs. I look; he stays. After a pause he kick-loops a metre or so
and grips the edge of the inside whitewashed wall. He feels or
checks quite slowly with the sock-shaped end of the near front
limb. His scrapers at the back are like square combs or harrows
neatly toothed. I know he is not thinking: "Where and what
the fuck is this?" But well he might if that is what he could.

6

God is there anything creamier than yogurt curds
with Monólithos mountain honey stirred right through?

Is there anything more grateful to the appetite
at half past noon and no one else in view?

I lick the plate, I lick the spoon again.
I do not doubt that you would do the same.

7

Gael, your skull is charred or ash; or in a lair
from Currie church interred (I wasn't there, and have
no details yet.) Your sensibility survives in all your
friends: your family of contact, near, dear or accidental.

Yesterday I thought I could detect the coastal shape
of Turkey; earlier in the week perhaps the outline
of a warship or patrol boat – grey, low slung along
the line of haze and sea. Politics and menace are always
there – even when we can hardly make them out.

8

Plimiri's the place I would go back to if I had the time and transport.
Not much more than a harbour shaded by an ugly concrete elevated
wall. Some genuine working boats. A couple of people casting from
the pier, and well along the curving beach two men with half a dozen
rods apiece fixed in shore gravel. Behind the sand, reed beds and
bamboo scrub. Just by the road, *Zoodohos Pigi* – 'the source of life'
the guidebook says – a sanctuary shut with bolts and boards at nearly
lunchtime Sunday. We think of asking for the key, but don't persist.

Adjacent (you can hear the voices in the kitchen) a 'seasonal taverna'
with a sloping graded bamboo screen roof. Out front the morning crop
of octopus draped over a clothesline. Inside, nothing fancy: *kalamari,*
bread, iced tea or a glass of beer. A couple of tentacles grilled up
quick. Bream or bass or snapper.

Nothing unusual and nothing out of place. A grim looking
Greek-American in a broad-brimmed hat comes padding in. A little
lag, and then his dreadful raucous wife. It makes no difference here –
not to us, not to several spindly lethal-looking cats, a local adonis
and his cheerful greasy friend, the happy-seeming cook-and-waitress
combined, her father or in-law absorbedly firing up the coals.

9

I just came back in after strolling round our strange *demesne*
in shorts and flip-flops, cheap Chinese panama, plus Calvin
Klein shades won in a raffle at work a week before we left.
Under a stumpy fig upon the barest patch of ground I drizzled
out libation to Apollo – assuming last-tap Heineken will
constitute libation.

Gael, I should have written you more letters in the past.
It would have done me good. No matter by train we were only
fifty minutes away. Can you see me now? You thought me
funny with my *immanental* and *transcendental*. So did I, of course;
though still believe the distinction happens to be true.

I put the insect out. It had imposed its strangeness long enough.
Outdoors has suddenly become more *personal* somehow – even if
that alien circumambient noise is only changed for me.

Here are the usual commonplaces: life is unfathomable.
Each existence only knows itself, and what it knows is mostly
dark and dull. The other insects near at hand make a noise
like scraping combs on table tops (or worse), and dowdy jays
add racket all around. Impenetrable, uncomforting, in various
ways we scrape and chafe and shift and shrill.

10

You know in Greece you cannot flush the paper –
you fold it and put it in a pail or bag to be discarded later.
This morning under the bag within the little plastic lidded
bin, securely wrapped, I lodged our passports and our money.
All week I had sought the perfect hiding place, so we could
take the air, nip for a swim, absent ourselves and set our
minds at ease. Well, rather late I've found it.

And in the placement added social commentary too.

11

In the time I've known him Augie's gone from bean-pot
penury to palpable acclaim. And though I know you know
that anyway, it just sounds good to say it.

At Monólithos we climbed through pines up cut stone steps
to reach St Panteleimon's church on top of Monopetra.
We made our way inside the scrubby though 'intact' holy
space with its scraggy icons, plastic bags. We fished and dried
five candles on a paper towel and brought them sputtering
to flame with matches, or – easier – sharing a light. We set
them back in the tin rectangular tray of sand and water
and blacked-out wicks had burned right down.

What did we wish for? What could we utter that might
safeguard the wee-est bit of what we are and love?
What could we do? What could I rightly say?

As I sat here, having worked myself up to tears to ask these
things (still bearing you in mind) a skinny bird, this *nondescript*,
comes to perch on the branch behind a big hibiscus. He cannot
reach the scarlet trumpet, nor its golden dusted tongue. He hops
and cocks and looks around. A coal tit without the coal. A blue tit
without the slightest trace of blue. If he were a humming-bird
he'd dive inside. He's not. Instead, he pecks away behind. I think
he may be trying to carve a back door in; but it's ants he's after,
ants he gets.

[I leave a pause here for you to say something back – perhaps
about the bird – perhaps about the flower. I'm sure about
the ants, by the way, because I looked there later.]

We do what we can. Illumination bobs right there
before your nose, and checks and pecks and flies away.
From time to time there's something rumbles louder, distant,
and when it comes carries a cliff-side off, and leaves the hotel
stranded, or buries half the town.

12

Please understand, there's nothing I would wish against
these placid, oddly *silent*, crowds that populate the beaches:
some gross, most semi-naked, some delectable. Nothing I would
wish to bear down merciless on them and their mild lubricities.
We all need rest and creature comfort. We all, though – and I take
the risk you'll disagree – to have a friend so well-disposed and
generous as you, it's tempting after all to say, yes that will do –
but *we all* can't stick with sun and sea, even in their amplitude;
or find in our failings and indulgences the subtlest support.

There's something else. There's something else – as you
could testify – that puts us under, pulls us back again; there's
something else in birds and birdlessness; something else we light
a candle for and place it in that dingy dish of wax and sand.

Rhodes-Glasgow
July/August 2004

SUONA PER TE

The bell strikes five from the tower of San Michele:
the seventeenth hour has slid away; a late September sun
has spilled along and off the south-faced wall, and soon this
beautiful, ravenous, vast city in the valley of the Po, its elegance
and industry, its desperate imprecations, the crowds that bay
and sway in the catafalque of San Siro, for Baggio, Shevchenko,
Zanzara, Volpone; intricate pinnacles and ladders of sound,
confections, conspiracies; *minna di vergine* on the *pasticcio*'s glass
counter shelf, somewhere with saffron *risotto al salto*, somewhere
a slit or truncheon, sirens and mayhem; all subtle, immediate
human exchanges – *come va? come sta?* or *vaffanculo* – matrons
encrusted in coral and amber, and anywhere, everywhere grace
of flesh and eyes and favour, *ragazze* with backpacks or Vuitton
or nothing; in a morning (God, *less* – take two stops on the metro)
perfection in appearance: innocent and wary, or down the stairs
in boots and hair, *meretrix* incarnate, blatant tits and vacant stare
(not *this* one), which even the dim or insensate must savour;
in the heart of the city, Stazione Centrale; O Santa Sofia, I've seen
your handmaidens, have worshipped abashed and chap-fallen;
dritto, sinistra, tenere la destra – what turn shall I take now? My soul
in the Duomo's half-dark disconcerted, so I light a tall candle;
dove dovrei girare? alas the sad pigeons adrift in the piazza, alas for
the clapped-out green nag under Pepe Missori; O Lucifer, your
handiwork and artisans are legion, in CISCO and Squawk Box
and NYMEX, Komatsu; excepting, no question, the white flat-
topped sisters, or by Porta Romana in *'the street of the orchards'*
Piera's *trattoria* (no nonsense, no menu, just stump up when she
asks you) – *carpaccio, tortino,* her *gnocchetti verdi*; O San Benedetto,
benedictions in return: each day, lips, tongue and throat slaked
by your watery benevolence; but all these, my brothers and sisters,
must founder: this night or next night we all will go under; if not
on the feast day of great San Michele, at four in the morning,
or in before lunchtime, or soon like the city in the hour that's
just struck now; shuttered or shadowless, in the flatlands
of Lombardy, Milano, unparalleled, lies down in the dark.

Acknowledgements

Thanks to the editors of the following, where some of these pieces first appeared:

Agenda; Ashen Meal (USA); *Chapman; Chelsea Hotel* (Germany); *Fras; Lines Review; Lallans; Notus* (USA); *Painted, spoken; Poetry Scotland; Schema* (Italy); *The Dark Horse* (Scotland/USA); *Zed 2O*.

"An Ounce of Wit to a Pound of Clergy" was published as a pamphlet by Minimal Missive Maximum Missile Publications: Edinburgh, 1991.

"Incantation" was printed in *Carmichael's Book* (Artbook/Morningstar: Inverness & Edinburgh 1997).

"Epitaph for a Butcher" was the title poem of *Epitaph for a Butcher* (Akros: Kirkcaldy, 1997), which also included "Excuse Me for Saying So," "Lady Scotter," "The Burnish," and "The Holt".

"Annals of Enlightenment" was printed in *Brilliant Cacophony* (The Scottish Sculpture Trust: Edinburgh, 1998).

"By the Beef and Not Touching It" was printed in *A Gathering for Gael Turnbull* (Vennel Press: Staines, 1998).

"Hole House Farm" was printed in *Love for Love* (pocketbooks: Edinburgh, 2000).

"Scota and Gaethelos" was printed in *Back to the Light* (Mariscat Press: Glasgow, 2001) with the following note:

"The legend of the founding of the Scottish people takes various meanders, some of which I've followed here, and some I've left alone. Gaedal Glas, they say, came from Greece to Egypt. His marriage to Scota, daughter of the Pharoah, is variously attributed to his daring and skill in arms, and to his skill in language. His comeliness is mentioned, as is his volatility. Before he died in what is now Galicia, he drove his sons to further exploration and settlement. In Walter Bower's medieval Scotichronicon *there is an image of Scota standing serenely in the stern of their ship as it sets out on the original westward voyage. My poem, I hope, anticipates not only the shaping of a nation, but the great gathering of folk on both banks of the Clyde. Nimrod, king in Scythia, ordered the building of what was to be known as the Tower of Babel".*

"Sparks in the Dark" was the title poem of *Sparks in the Dark* (Akros: Kirkcaldy, 2002), which also included "Above Stromness," "Alba," *"Coup de Foudre,"* "Cunty Fingers," "Heading in to the Bar," "Hippertie-Skippertie," "Jimp," "Landing," "No, No," "She Said," "Sibilance: Swifts," "The Hat" and "West Coast Tally".

The epigraph for "Carbon Atom" is quoted from commentary text for posters from "Powers of Ten" created by the Eames Office.

"A Saturno Conditum" was engraved in stone and mounted in the town of Arpino, Italy in 2002 as part of the international project *Il Libro di Pietra*. The full motto *"Arpinum a Saturno conditum"* is translated: "Arpino, founded by Saturn".

"Epistle from Pevkos" was issued as a pamphlet from Link-light: Glasgow, 2004. The tsunami in the Indian Ocean came later that same year in December.